I Can Predict,
I Won't Be Tricked!

Bridget Pederson

Consulting Editors, Diane Craig, M.A./Reading Specialist
and Susan Kosel, M.A. Education

Published by ABDO Publishing Company, 4940 Viking Drive, Edina, Minnesota 55435.

Printed in the United States.

Credits
Edited by: Pam Price
Curriculum Coordinator: Nancy Tuminelly
Cover and Interior Design and Production: Mighty Media
Photo Credits: BananaStock Ltd., Brand X Pictures, Kelly Doudna, Image100, Photodisc, ShutterStock,
Stockbyte, Wewerka Photography

Library of Congress Cataloging-in-Publication Data

Pederson, Bridget.
    I can predict, I won't be tricked! / Bridget Pederson.
      p. cm. -- (Science made simple)
    ISBN 10 1-59928-582-7 (hardcover)
    ISBN 10 1-59928-583-5 (paperback)

    ISBN 13 978-1-59928-582-5 (hardcover)
    ISBN 13 978-1-59928-583-2 (paperback)
    1. Induction (Logic)--Juvenile literature. 2. Forecasting--Juvenile literature. I. Title.

    BC91.P43 2007
    153.4'32--dc22

                                                                                2006022489

SandCastle Level: Transitional

SandCastle™ books are created by a professional team of educators, reading specialists, and content developers around
five essential components—phonemic awareness, phonics, vocabulary, text comprehension, and fluency—to assist young
readers as they develop reading skills and strategies and increase their general knowledge. All books are written,
reviewed, and leveled for guided reading, early reading intervention, and Accelerated Reader® programs for use in
shared, guided, and independent reading and writing activities to support a balanced approach to literacy instruction.
The SandCastle™ series has four levels that correspond to early literacy development. The levels help teachers and
parents select appropriate books for young readers.

Emerging Readers
(no flags)

Beginning Readers
(1 flag)

Transitional Readers
(2 flags)

Fluent Readers
(3 flags)

These levels are meant only as a guide. All levels are subject to change.

To **predict** is to guess what you think will happen in the future. A prediction is based on information you already know or things that you observe.

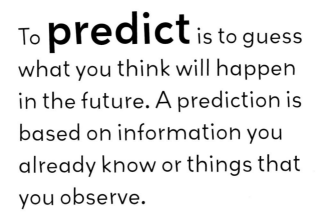

Words used to talk about predicting:
information
observe

There are dark  in the sky.

I predict that it will  today.

The on the tree are and .

I predict that the  will fall soon.

The ☀ is shining and it's 40 degrees outside.

I predict that the

will melt soon.

I Can Predict, I Won't Be Tricked!

Rita's brother
is a funny guy.
He thought he'd give
this trick a try.

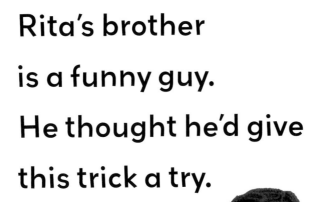

A trick is not
always cool.
Be careful about
who you fool!

He says, "Rita, have a look through the binoculars that are near the book."
Rita sees shoe polish on the floor.
She thinks she's seen this once before.

It's good to think things through before you decide what to do.

13

Rita has heard
of this trick before.
She heard it from
her friend next door.
So Rita can predict.
She tells her brother,
"I won't be tricked!"

Rita is very wise.
She has saved herself
from black marks
around her eyes.

Predicting Every Day!

Ariel and her mom read a story about a lost dog that wandered away from home.

Based on information given in the book, Ariel predicts that the dog will find its way home.

17

There is only a minute left, and Isaac's team is winning by ten points.

Isaac predicts they will win the game.

Emily and Paige know that ice cream can melt.

They predict that the ice cream will melt in the sun if they don't eat it fast enough.

Diego looks out the window and observes that the trees are waving. Diego predicts it's windy outside.

What can you predict by looking out your window?

Glossary

binoculars – a magnifying device you look through with both eyes to get a better look at things that are far away.

information – the facts known about an event or subject.

observe – to watch carefully.

polish – a paste that is rubbed on a surface to make it shiny and protect it from damage. Some things we polish are shoes, furniture, and cars.

wander – to walk around without knowing where you want to go.